When I get

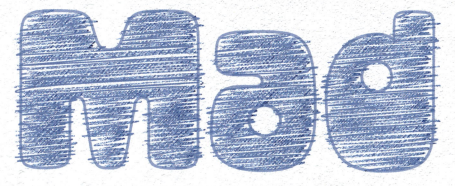

Written By: Julie Grapes
Illustrated By: Celeste Santiago

My name is Jonah,
and this is how I look when I get mad.

My face may be different from time to time, depending on what has upset me and how mad I am.

Sometimes,
I get so mad that it feels like smoke comes out of my ears.

As I start to get mad,
my face will slowly start to get red.

As my face gets redder and redder,
I start to feel really hot.

Sometimes,
I look like a tomato that's ready
to explode.

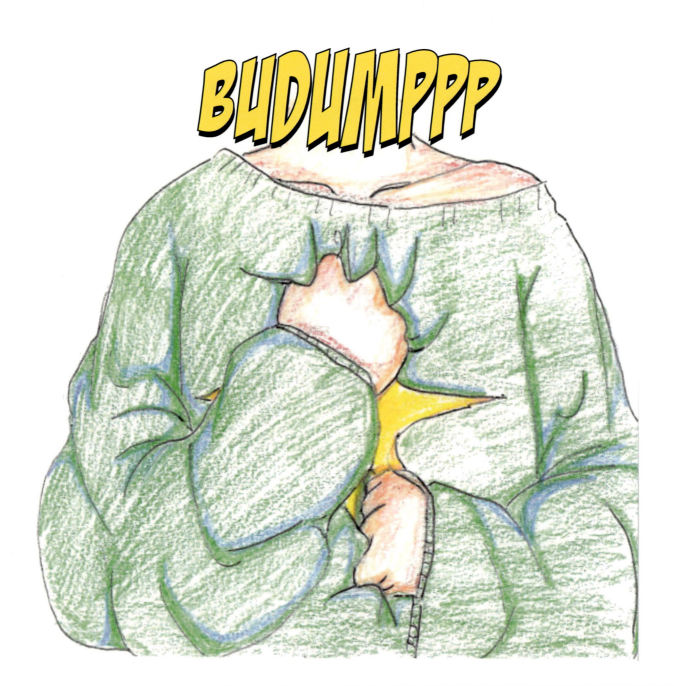

My heartbeat
will start to quicken;

it almost feels like
my heart is coming out
of my chest.

I have learned some ways
to calm down when I start to
feel angry.

I can draw pictures
and color them.

When I get mad,
I will try taking deep breaths first.

Taking in deep breaths
brings more oxygen to the brain
and helps my body slowly calm down.

When I am calm,
I feel better and have more energy
to play with my family and friends in a
positive way.

I like to do puzzles,
so my mom suggested that
I choose a puzzle to work on as
I calm down

I get so involved
with the Puzzle that
I forget why I was so mad.

When the weather is nice,
I will go outside and jump
on my trampoline.

Physical exercise helps
release chemicals in the body
called endorphins that
make you happy.

I can even go to my room when I get mad and scream into my pillows.

When I scream into my pillows, I am able to get rid of some of the anger that I feel.

When screaming into
my pillows doesn't work,
I will punch and hit my pillows.

I feel better after a few minutes.
Afterwards, I will lie down and cuddle
into my pillows and relax
until I am ready to go and talk
to Mom.

Once I calm down,
I can talk to my family.

My family may be able
to help me find a solution to
what is bothering me.

I know if I try really hard,
I will learn my coping skills
and always be safe.

The End

Made in the USA
Middletown, DE
12 August 2024